A Caring Heart

Vonette Zachary Bright

NewLife
PUBLICATIONS

My Heart in His Hands Bible Study: A Caring Heart

Published by
NewLife Publications
A ministry of Campus Crusade for Christ
P.O. Box 620877
Orlando, FL 32862-0877

ISBN 1-56399-181-0

Design and production by Genesis Group

Cover design by Koechel Peterson & Associates, Inc., Minneapolis, MN

Printed in the United States of America

Unless otherwise indicated, Scripture quotations are from the *New International Version*, © 1973, 1978, 1984 by the International Bible Society. Published by Zondervan Bible Publishers, Grand Rapids, Michigan.

For more information, write:

L.I.F.E., Campus Crusade for Christ—P.O. Box 40, Flemington Markets, 2129, Australia

Campus Crusade for Christ of Canada—Box 529, Sumas, WA 98295

Campus Crusade for Christ—Fairgate House, King's Road, Tyseley, Birmingham, B11 2AA, United Kingdom

Lay Institute for Evangelism, Campus Crusade for Christ—P.O. Box 8786, Auckland, 1035, New Zealand

Campus Crusade for Christ—9 Lock Road #3-03, PacCan Centre, Singapore

Great Commission Movement of Nigeria—P.O. Box 500, Jos, Plateau State, Nigeria, West Africa

Campus Crusade for Christ International—100 Lake Hart Drive, Orlando, FL 32832, USA

Contents

My Dear Friends

I want to welcome you to this Bible study series for women! I'm excited about the opportunity to walk through the Scriptures with you as we explore all that God's Word has for the busy woman of today.

Every unique detail of a woman's life fits into a grand and glorious plan. My prayer is that women of all ages will desire to have a deeper relationship with God, and to discover the joys of knowing Him and His plan for their lives.

God's Word speaks so directly to every aspect of a woman's life. It fills us with wisdom, imparts God's love, and provides ample instructions for our daily walk. The Scriptures tell us the results we can expect when we live in agreement with God's plan, and what we can expect if we do not live as He directs.

The Bible has much to say about its value and relevance for our lives today. It gives us guidance: "Your word is a lamp to my feet and a light for my path" (Psalm 119:105). It gives understanding: "The unfolding of your words gives light; it gives understanding to the simple" (Psalm 119:130). It is not made up of cold, dead words, but living, Spirit-filled words that can affect our hearts and our lives: "For the word of God is living and active. Sharper than any double-edged sword, it penetrates even to dividing soul and spirit, joints and marrow; it judges the thoughts and attitudes of the heart" (Hebrews 4:12).

When I wrote the devotional books for the series *My Heart In His Hands*, it was with the desire to encourage women and to help them realize that God is interested and involved in the details of their lives. My goal was to provide a practical and systematic way for a woman to examine her heart and recognize how beautifully God has created her. This set of study guides has been designed to complement each seasonal devotional.

Each study guide has been developed prayerfully and can be used for individual or group study. Perhaps you are part of a group that meets regularly to study and discuss the precious treasures of God's Word. I have been a part of such groups for many years, and I am still overjoyed to meet with these women.

Whether you will study on your own or with others, it is my heartfelt prayer that you will open your heart to His Word and enjoy the blessing of resting confidently in His hands.

From my heart to yours,

Vonette Z. Bright

How to Use This Study

The *My Heart in His Hands* Bible study series is designed for the busy woman who desires a deeper walk with God. The twenty lessons in *A Caring Heart* embrace the glorious truth that the God who cares for us helps us to love and care for others as we walk with Him.

A Caring Heart provides everything you need to understand biblical principles and use them to transform your life. Whether you are working hard at your career, involved in full-time ministry, knee-deep in preschoolers, or raising teenagers, you can find the time to complete the short lessons and receive encouragement for your day. The questions require less time than most courses so that you can fit Bible study into your hectic schedule. The refreshing look at Scripture passages will help you apply God's Word to your daily needs.

You can use this book as an individual study during your quiet time with God, or as a group study with other women. (A Discussion Guide with answers to the Bible questions is located at the back of this book to help a group facilitator.) It can also be used as a companion to the *My Heart in His Hands* devotional series.

The book contains an in-depth look at the lives of two women: a biblical portrait of a godly woman and an inspirational portrait of an outstanding contemporary woman. These portraits, woven throughout the book, give insights into a caring heart.

Each lesson includes these parts:

- His Word—a Scripture passage to read
- Knowing His Heart—understanding God's Word
- Knowing My Heart—personal questions to consider
- My Heart in His Hands—a timely quote to ponder

Whether to start your morning or end your day, you can use this study to focus on God's Word and on His marvelous works in your life. As you apply these principles, you will truly nourish your caring heart!

A Caring Heart

Have you ever taken a young child to the zoo? One of the favorite animals for most children is the elephant. The amazing thing about elephants is how much they care for each other. They live in family units under the guidance of a mature female. They caress each other with their trunks and trumpet a warning when they see danger.

Elephants even grieve over the death of a friend. They bury their dead by piling leaves and twigs over the body, then stay by the "grave" for hours.

God gave many animals an instinct for caring. How much more must God expect us, those who are made in His image, to care for others!

But many things get in the way of our caring actions. We're too busy or too tired. We withhold our kindness when it's unappeciated. We don't know how to comfort people, so we just ignore their problems.

Imagine this scenario: You get a call from the emergency room telling you that your daughter has been in a car accident. She's in critical condition and may not make it.

As you rush to the hospital, you begin praying. "Oh, God, please protect my daughter. Bring her safely through this terrible ordeal."

But God doesn't answer. He's thinking, *I don't know what to say to My child during a crisis like this, so I'll just let her work it out on her own.*

We can't imagine God responding to us in that way. And He never would. His caring heart feels our pain and soothes our hurts. He is so involved in our lives that He sent Jesus in the form of a man so that He could feel, be tempted, ache, cry, laugh, grieve, and become exhausted just as we do. God knows what we feel, and He responds with His care whenever we need Him. Then He expects us to pass His caring heart on to others.

Although most believers would say that they care for others, our human efforts at caring are often shallow and awkward. True caring is learned only at the feet of Jesus.

Some aspects of caring may come natural for you. Perhaps you are generous with your finances when you see a need, or you like to listen to people who are hurting. Yet we each have areas in our lives where we have no room for caring, so God cannot bless us or use us there. Perhaps you hesitate to hug that squalling baby in the church nursery, or you can't stand the smell of that lonely old man who has no one to care for him. And your heart turns to jelly when you have to comfort someone who has just lost a loved one.

I encourage you to use the lessons in this book as a journal for building a caring lifestyle. Jot down places where you might fortify your caring heart. Make notes on areas that you feel are your strengths and through which God may be calling you to serve more frequently.

Caring always leaves the giver more blessed than the receiver. We may experience heartache and pain when our care is rejected or when people accept it ungratefully. But more often, we will discover new friends, build closer relationships, and communicate at deeper levels with those we reach out to in love.

As you place your heart in God's hands, ask Him to fill it with His caring Spirit.

The Heart of Dorcas

The candlelight flickers in the comfortably cool room. The garment is just about finished. Calluses on the tender hands sewing it tell of the many garments stitched before this one. The woman coughs and wipes her damp forehead with a cloth. *When did it get so hot in here?* she wonders. *Maybe I'm coming down with an illness.* Nevertheless, she wants to finish this garment. Tomorrow she will be delivering baskets of clothing and food to the poor widows living in the ghetto.

The next morning, the woman rises with the sun. As she leaves her house with baskets in hand, she shakes off her chill and gathers her shawl around her small shoulders.

As usual, the city has awakened early. She passes through the market area, where merchants and shoppers are engaged in the day's business. As she approaches the ghetto, the dwellings become smaller and more run-down. The air is dustier and has a distinct odor of masses of humanity crammed into a small space. The people are dressed in dirty, ragged garments.

Finally, the woman reaches her destination—a small dwelling, more like a shanty-tent on the side of a larger building. She calls into the skin-covered opening, "Hello, Mara. It's me, Dorcas."

As the covering parts, a frail middle-aged woman pokes her head out and says softly, "Oh, Dorcas. So good to see you."

Dorcas hands one of the baskets to Mara. "I brought this basket for you. It's not much, but with winter coming, I know you and the children will need some warm clothing."

Mara looks at the basket, then up at Dorcas, tears in her eyes. "Oh... you are too kind... I can't accept this... It's too much."

"Please," Dorcas responds, "I would like you to have it. It gives me great joy to do this for you and the children."

Mara looks into Dorcas's eyes and sees that she truly means what she says. "All right," Mara says finally, "Thank you very much for your kindness. It means more than you will ever know. Won't you please come in and have some tea?"

"Thank you for the kind offer," Dorcas says gratefully, "but I must deliver this other basket. And I am feeling a bit under the weather."

With a final wave farewell, she trots down the road to her next stop.

Although we can only speculate about the life Dorcas lived, we can imagine that scenes such as this were repeated many times in her life. As with us today, she was faced with the opportunity to give generously to those in need.

Acts 9 tells us that Dorcas was "always doing good and helping the poor," even up to the time she became ill and died. Her death was more than those around her could bear. When Peter arrived, he found her body surrounded by loved ones and those touched by her generosity. Through God's Spirit and power, Peter brought Dorcas back to life.

The caring heart is one of humility, generosity, and compassion. But this heart does not come from the fleshly nature. It comes only through God's Spirit working in our lives. Dorcas allowed His Spirit full reign in her life. And just look at the people she touched. Today's woman could do no less—with His power.

The Heart of Amy Carmichael

When Amy Carmichael was 16 years old, her mother took her to a Belfast teashop. While sipping tea and sampling sweets, Amy noticed a little face pressed against the window. *How charming,* she thought, *to see a little girl peering in at the sweets.* But when leaving the teashop, Amy saw that the girl's dress was thin and dirty. With a shock Amy realized that the ragamuffin girl was hungry and barefoot on a cold, drizzly day! *Oh, how could I have thought there was any charm in being so desperately poor?* she lamented.

In the cozy warmth of her bedroom that night, she set her feelings to verse:

> When I grow up and money have, I know what I will do,
> I'll build a great big lovely place for little girls like you.

Amy was born in Ireland on December 16, 1867, the oldest of seven children. Her father ran a flour mill, and the Carmichaels lived in one of the largest houses in Millisle.

When she was older, Amy was sent to a boarding school in England. In 1884, as she sang in the choir at the meetings of the Children's Special Service Mission, a familiar hymn touched her heart profoundly. "Jesus loves me! This I know, for the Bible tells me so." She writes of this experience, "I opened my heart to Him and in His great mercy the Good Shepherd has drawn me into His fold!" Her exciting Christian journey had begun.

The first stop on her journey was the Belfast City Mission. Amy invited many children to come, sing, have fun, and study God's Word. Soon, she had Bible studies and prayer groups for both boys and girls. Amy's meetings grew to such large numbers that she eventually had to build her own hall. A prefabricated sheet metal building became the new Welcome Hall. Word of her successful ministry spread, and she was invited to start another Welcome Hall in Manchester.

After her father died, Amy lived in the home of family friend and surrogate father, Robert Wilson, for two years. She continued ministering at the Children's Special Service Mission, where children flocked to her in such numbers that Bible classes had to be added.

Soon, Amy felt a great need to "go forth" to evangelize the world. In March 1893, she sailed east to Japan. She had to leave Japan after a year for health reasons, and eventually God led her to Dohnavur, India.

In 1901, a Christian brought to Amy a seven-year-old girl, Preena, who was to become a "woman of the temple." (Some Indian families gave their young children for service in Hindu temples. "Temple children" were subjected to unimaginable acts.) Preena referred to Amy as "Amma" or mother. Amy was to become "mother" to many forsaken temple children.

By 1919, her ministry, The Dohnavur Fellowship, had twenty nurseries. Eventually, the Fellowship acquired other property for various facilities, including a hospital.

Amy consistently tried to die to herself to let God be all—in and through her. The caring and compassion demonstrated by her life began at a teashop with her mother. She did indeed "build a great big lovely place for little girls like you."

Source: Sam Wellman, *Amy Carmichael: A Life Abandoned to God* (Uhrichsville, OH: Barbour Publishing), 1988.

PART 1

The Heart of Caring

In the Old Testament, the heart is described as the center of a person's being. It was more than the symbol of romantic love. Instead, the heart stood for a person's emotions, thinking, spirit, and was even linked to the physical life.

Scripture uses the word heart many times. For example, when Hannah prays in 1 Samuel 2:1, "My heart rejoices in the LORD," she was describing more than an emotion of joy. Instead, with every part of her being, she delighted in God. That's why she was willing to give her only son to God's service in the temple when he was a child. She had already given God all she had. Her actions were just an outpouring of her heart attitude.

A common phrase today is, "Put your heart into it!" That

means giving more than outward effort, but acting with all you are to accomplish the task.

What kind of caring do you expect when God says He cares for you? (See 1 Peter 5:7.) I'm sure you expect more than an emotional response. We want God to care for us with all of His eternal, wondrous attributes. His caring encompasses His love, compassion, and comfort—His "heart." We can count on His justice, righteousness, and mercy.

That's what makes God's heart of caring so complete. He cannot care with just a part of His nature; He cares for us with "every fiber of His being."

As fallen humans, however, we tend to compartmentalize our "hearts." On Sunday we "care" for our church friends. On Monday, we forget about them and take up the cause for someone at work. At the nail salon, we "care" for the manicurist by listening to her and giving soothing advice. But after walking out the door, we get busy and don't think of her problems again until our next appointment.

Just think if God cared for us only when it was convenient for Him. A heart of caring implies that we are involved with someone with our whole being, whenever it is needed.

Of course, as flesh and blood, we cannot be everything to everyone at all times. It's impossible, and if we try, we will burn ourselves out. That's why it's so important for us to meet regularly with the Lord. He will direct us to the needs He wants us to meet. Our eyes must be open to needs around us and to opportunities to show His caring heart as He leads. Then we must care with our whole hearts.

Wholehearted caring is shown through so many ways. In Part 1, we'll examine love and generosity and how God demonstrates these qualities for us. Then we will consider how we can demonstrate these qualities to reflect His caring heart.

Christ's Love for Us

It was the greatest lesson on love ever given on earth. He left heaven to be born as a baby in a manger. He grew up as a child of hard-working, loving parents. At age 30, He began His ministry, humbly serving the people and preaching a message of repentance and redemption. At the young age of 33, He willingly gave up His life to be crucified on a cross, a sin offering for the sins of mankind. And three days later, He was gloriously resurrected to enable all of us to have victory over death. Christ did all of these things for one reason—He loves us. Because of His great love and sacrifice, we can be redeemed from our sins. And through His love we are truly able to love others.

His WORD: 1 John 4:19–21

KNOWING His HEART

1. According to verse 19, why should we love others?

2. What is the proof of our love for God (verse 20)?

3. Why could we conclude that a person does not love God?

4. What is the command given to us in verse 21?

KNOWING *My* HEART

1. Name several ways God has demonstrated His love for you.

2. Describe a time when you demonstrated love for a fellow believer. What were the results?

3. To whom do you have the hardest time demonstrating God's love? Why?

4. This week, how can you live out Christ's command to love?

My HEART IN *His* HANDS

"Christ has not only spoken to us by his life but has also spoken for us by his death."

—SÖREN KIERKEGAARD

LESSON 2

The Importance of Generosity

People around us have many problems for which they need assistance. Here are just a few. Material needs: about 750,000 Americans are homeless on any given night. Emotional needs: some form of depression affects about 19 million Americans each year. Physical needs: about 1.3 million new cases of cancer were diagnosed in 2001. Spiritual needs: 59 percent of Americans do not have a personal relationship with Jesus Christ. The question we ought to ask ourselves is, What can we do for those around us to make their problems a little easier? God has given each of us blessings, which we can share with others. He encourages us to do so, and He blesses through our willing generosity and service in His name.

His **WORD:** 2 Corinthians 9:6–15

KNOWING *His* HEART

1. What do verses 6–8 tell us about giving?

2. What role does God play in our giving (verses 10 and 11)?

3. What are two purposes of generosity (verse 12)?

4. How does our generosity become a witness for God?

KNOWING *My* HEART

1. What are the primary needs of people in your neighborhood? In your church?

2. How can you meet at least one of those needs with what God has given you?

3. How has God demonstrated generosity to you?

4. How does your life demonstrate "the surpassing grace God has given you"?

My HEART IN *His* HANDS

"Jesus does not expect perfection, but he wants us to give ourselves wholeheartedly."
—J. HEINRICH ARNOLD

LESSON 3

A Heart of Love

In 1 John 4:16 we read, "God is love. Whoever lives in love lives in God, and God in him." Love is one of the characteristics of God, and when we show love to others through our actions, we demonstrate a characteristic of the God who lives in us. When we give to someone in need, without concern about recognition or reciprocation, we are demonstrating graciousness that comes only from God. In this lesson, we will read about the Parable of the Good Samaritan. With this story, Jesus went beyond the letter of the Law to the spirit of the Law. True Christian character is more than simply doing what is right; it means having a heart of love to go beyond the rules and expectations and selflessly help a person in need.

His **WORD:** Luke 10:25–37

KNOWING *His* **HEART**

1. Why do you think an expert was questioning Jesus (verse 25)?

2. What main principle is this parable illustrating (verse 27)?

3. What did it cost the Samaritan to help the wounded man? What did he expect in return?

4. When Jesus said, "Go and do likewise," to what was He referring?

KNOWING *My* HEART

1. Which is most difficult: to love the Lord with all your heart, soul, strength, and mind, or to love your neighbor as yourself? Why?

2. Search your heart and ask yourself: What would I have done if I had encountered the injured man?

3. Describe an occasion when you had mercy on someone who needed it.

4. Specifically, how can you extend mercy to people who are hard to love?

My HEART IN *His* HANDS

"It is impossible to be truly converted to God without being thereby converted to our neighbor."

—JOHN R. W. STOTT

LESSON 4

Acts of Love

There is a type of wristwatch that has a clear casing, allowing the inner workings to be seen. Visible through the clear case is the "real" watch, the parts that do the work of keeping time. The exterior elements are merely cosmetic. When the outside is transparent, the inside action can be seen as the watch hands move as they were designed to. Most watches, however, don't have this see-through casing; all we know is that the watch keeps time. The Holy Spirit living within the Christian should be visible to those around us through our transparent spirit and through the acts of Christian love that we live out.

His **WORD:** 1 John 3:11–24

KNOWING *His* HEART

1. What is the difference between a person who remains spiritually dead and one who has eternal life (verse 11–15)?

2. According to verses 17 and 18, how can we show the sacrificial love spoken of in verse 16?

3. What are the benefits of demonstrating our love by our actions (verses 19 and 20)?

4. What two things did Jesus command us to do (verse 23)?

KNOWING *My* HEART

1. How can you "lay down your life" for your Christian brother or sister in your daily activities?

2. In what ways has your heart condemned you for failing to relay God's love to others?

3. How does the phrase "God is greater than our hearts" apply to your answer above?

4. How does verse 24 help you to know that Christ lives in you?

My HEART IN *His* HANDS

"Be kind, for everyone you meet is fighting a great battle."
—PHILO OF ALEXANDRIA

LESSON 5

The Attractiveness of Caring

A life of love and generosity is like a sweet nectar; it attracts people. If you set out something sweet in the garden, in no time it will be visited by honeybees looking for food to bring back to their hive. If you plant certain types of flowers, you will also attract bees. And their honey will take on the flavor of whatever you plant. If you have an orange orchard, the honey will take on the blossoms' delicate essence. Dorcas had a sweet spirit that drew people to her. Her caring hands made gifts for the needy, and those gifts were the honey that brought all kinds of people to her. Her selfless acts were noticed by others who responded to her caring spirit. In fact, we could say that her love was infectious and changed the lives of others for good.

His WORD: Acts 9:36–42

KNOWING *His* HEART

1. What evidence does this passage give about the kind of person Dorcas was?

2. What happened to Dorcas and how did her friends respond (verses 37 and 38)?

3. What did Peter see when he arrived at the home of Dorcas (verse 39)?

4. What did Peter do for Dorcas (verses 40 and 41)?

KNOWING *My* HEART

1. Who do you know with a caring heart like Dorcas? What kind of influence does this person have?

2. What excuses do people give for not helping the poor and needy? Which are valid and which aren't?

3. How have people been attracted to your acts of caring?

4. In what ways would you like to increase your service to the poor and needy?

My HEART IN *His* HANDS

"Christ's ministry to this impoverished, captive, blinded and oppressed world must, in one way or another, also be ours."

—KAREN BURTON MAINS

PART 2

The Role of Caring

We've all seen lives exemplified by selfless caring: the Sunday school teacher of special-education students; the group who visits convalescent home patients; the child who makes breakfast in bed for her sick mother.

Ray's wife, in her fifties, was diagnosed with breast cancer. The news was a blow, but they both put the future in God's hands. Chemotherapy devastated Jeanie. She was thin and gaunt and soon lost all her hair. Her clothes hung on her frame, and her eyes looked sunken.

She recovered from the first bout of chemotherapy, but then discovered that the cancer had spread to her bones. She endured another round of treatments, then some time later, a third one. Her face looked aged and she wore hats to cover her bald head.

She walked with a cane because her leg bones were so weak.

But her tragedy exposed the caring heart of her husband. The tenderness with which her husband cared for her was touching. It wasn't just his gentleness and thoughtfulness that moved people's hearts, it was the love in his eyes. As he sat beside her in the pew, he would look at her as if she were the most beautiful woman in the world. His arm softly caressed her back throughout the service. His caring heart taught just as much of God's truth as the sermon did.

Caring was at the heart of Jesus' earthly ministry. Of course, His caring was demonstrated by His death, but also through all His actions. Consider the people He touched: lepers, filthy with an untouchable disease; prostitutes, shunned by others because of their lifestyle; tax collectors, hated by their neighbors because of their greed; Judas, the one Jesus knew would betray Him.

How many "untouchables" are part of your life or ministry? Are you exposing your caring heart through the kinds of people you love, the actions you choose, the words you say? Or are you caring only for those who are easy to befriend? We all find it easy to love those who are kind to us or who reciprocate our kindness. But it is much harder to be like Jesus and reach out to those whom society has rejected.

Another group Jesus cared about were the religious rulers. He knew how much they hated Him, and that the result of their hatred would be His crucifixion. Yet He spent time discussing God's ways with them. No one can accuse Jesus of not giving them an opportunity to reject their ways of thinking and accept Him. In the Book of Acts, we find that some of these leaders did receive Jesus Christ as their Messiah.

In Part 2, we will study God's heart of love and compassion and Christ's ministry of caring. Then we will discover our responsibility for doing good and the role that our own suffering plays in the comfort of others.

LESSON 6

God's Love and Compassion

Why does God care for us? It's not because that is what He *does*. God cares for us because that is who He *is*. Love, compassion, and caring are such an integral part of who He is that He can't help caring for us. God has the amazing, incomprehensible ability not only to watch over tribes and nations, but to watch over each individual. He cares as much about your concerns as He does about those of a state or nation. He lovingly created us in His own image. He graciously provided a Savior to redeem us from our sins. And He patiently waits for us to receive His love and the fullness of the blessings He has for us. In Psalm 116, we will find the praises of one whose cry to God was heard. Be comforted in knowing that the same God is available to you.

His **WORD:** Psalm 116:1–7

KNOWING *His* **HEART**

1. Why does the psalmist love the Lord?

2. Describe the psalmist's distress in verse 3.

3. What attributes of God are described in verses 5 and 6?

4. According to verse 7, why can the psalmist be at rest?

KNOWING *My* HEART

1. What cries could you bring to the Lord's ear today?

2. How has God demonstrated graciousness, righteousness, and compassion in your life?

3. What does it mean to be "simplehearted"? How can you strive to be simplehearted?

4. In what ways does God help you to be "at rest once more"?

My HEART IN *His* HANDS

"Jesus went out of His way to embrace the unloved and unworthy, the folks who matter not at all to the rest of society—they embarrass us, we wish they'd go away—to prove that even 'nobodies' matter infinitely to God."
—PHILIP YANCEY

LESSON 7

Christ's Ministry of Caring

"**J**esus wept." Those two words from John 11:35 succinctly describe the heart of Christ. Jesus, the Son of God, had all the power of heaven and earth at His command. Yet He had the tenderness of heart to weep over the death of His friend Lazarus. However, Christ's compassion did not end with His emotions. He took action. He went to Lazarus' tomb and spoke life into His friend's body. Lazarus arose and walked from death to life. Christ's life on earth continually provides us with examples of a caring heart in action. As followers of Christ, we can show Christ to the world when we turn our sympathetic hearts toward service to others. The opportunities for ministry are all around us.

His WORD: Mark 5:21–34

KNOWING *His* HEART

1. What was wrong with the woman in this story?

2. Why did the woman touch Jesus' cloak (verse 27 and 28)?

3. How did Jesus show His great sensitivity in verses 30 and 31?

4. According to verses 32–34, how did Jesus meet the woman's need?

KNOWING *My* HEART

1. What have you learned about Jesus' ministry of caring from today's lesson?

2. How can you be more sensitive to the needs of others?

3. In what ways has God healed wounds from which you suffer?

4. What part did your faith in Jesus play in your healing?

My HEART IN *His* HANDS

"It is your living faith in the adequacy of the One who is in you, which releases His divine action through you."
—W. IAN THOMAS

LESS⊕N 8

Our Responsibility to Do Good

"Let us do good to all people." This is the apostle Paul's admonishment to us in Galatians 6:10. How do we live out this idea in the real world? How do we act toward the person who recklessly cuts us off in traffic, the telemarketers who relentlessly call at dinnertime and won't take no for an answer, the Little League parent who shamelessly scolds our son for missing a play? We want to lash out at people who irritate us. In our own strength, we can never respond to people the way God wants us to respond. This fact is reiterated each day that we live and work in a fallen world. It is only through the power of God's Spirit working in us that we can truly "do good to all people."

His **WORD:** Galatians 6:1–10

KNOWING *His* **HEART**

1. What are we to do when dealing with someone caught in a sin (verse 1)?

2. According to verses 3–5, how should we view ourselves in relation to others?

3. Describe the principle of sowing and reaping (verses 7 and 8).

4. Why should we continue to do good (verse 9)?

KNOWING *My* HEART

1. Why is it important for someone to restore you gently if you stray into sin?

2. Take time to "examine your own work." How does it compare to God's standard?

3. How have you sown to your flesh? How can you sow to the Spirit in these areas?

4. How do you feel when you do good to others? What have you reaped from these seeds of kindness?

My HEART IN *His* HANDS

"Holy Spirit, think through me till your ideas are my ideas."
—AMY CARMICHAEL

LESSON 9

The Role of Suffering and Comfort

People often become involved in a cause when it affects them or someone they love. Carroll O'Connor began anti-drug crusades when his son died of a drug overdose. Michael J. Fox took up the cause of Parkinson's disease when he was diagnosed with the illness. There is something about experiencing a grief, an illness, a separation, or any other trial that draws us to people who are suffering with the same problem. When we go through these trials, God comforts us. Then we, in turn, can comfort those who are coming along behind us. As Christians, we have more than medical cures for disease or therapy for sorrows. We can point hurting people to the arms of our heavenly Father because we know how comforting they are.

His **WORD:** 2 Corinthians 1:3–7

KNOWING *His* **HEART**

1. Why are we able to comfort those who are in trouble (verses 3 and 4)?

2. How are suffering and comfort related in verse 5?

3. How can those in the Body of Christ affect others (verse 6)?

4. What is the hope we find in verse 7?

KNOWING *My* HEART

1. How has God been the "Father of compassion and the God of all comfort" in your life?

2. How have you suffered for the cause of Christ and His Church?

3. In what ways have you received comfort that you can pass on to others?

4. How has past suffering produced patience in your life?

My HEART IN *His* HANDS

"When we are attempting to comfort one who is suffering, our first priority should be to strengthen his or her faith and not to give pat answers."
—DANIEL J. SEMUNDSON

LESSON 10

The Caring Principle

Most Christians have read about the godly character of Dorcas and her heart of caring. But her story also emphasizes another person's caring heart: Peter's. Peter responded to the accounts of Dorcas's good works by doing a supernatural act—raising her from the dead! This highlights a principle found throughout Scripture—caring acts by one person reproduce caring acts in those around them. Dorcas's good deeds set in motion a series of kind acts. First was Dorcas, then those who loved her took care of her body and sent for Peter. Next, these people showed Peter all that Dorcas had done. Then Peter raised her from the dead. Is your life causing gentle ripples of kindness around you? Caring deeds won't always result in more kind acts. But when they do, many will see Christ through our actions.

His **WORD:** Acts 9:32–42

KNOWING *His* HEART

1. How does Peter care for the man Aeneas (verses 33,34)?

2. Why did the disciples send for Peter to come to Dorcas?

3. What does verse 40 reveal about how God works?

4. How did this event affect the city of Joppa (verse 42)?

KNOWING *My* HEART

1. How has someone passed a caring heart on to you?

2. How have you seen a caring heart passed on to others?

3. Caring acts of Dorcas and Amy Carmichael led people to believe in Jesus. How does this encourage you?

4. Specifically, how can you use the caring principle to tell others about Jesus?

My HEART IN *His* HANDS

"First, I thank my God through Jesus Christ for all of you, because [the report of] your faith is made known to all the world and is commended everywhere."

—ROMANS 1:8 (*AMPLIFIED*)

PART 3

The Acts of Caring

As believers in Christ, we have numerous opportunities to participate in acts of caring. One Sunday school class was given an opportunity to show Christ's love when a tragedy happened to a class member. Mike's wife, Caroline, had suffered with depression for years. One day their family went camping. She told her husband that she wasn't feeling well and wanted to return home. "Go ahead and stay," she said. "Bring our son back with you tomorrow. He won't want to miss out on the fun."

Mike had no idea that she had fallen into a deep depression; she had hidden her feelings well. When he and their son came home the next morning, he found Caroline in bed, dead from an overdose of drugs. His life was plunged into chaos.

That's when the class went into action. Although Mike wasn't a faithful attender, the members pitched in to help him. He had little money for funeral expenses, so they held a car wash and donated from their personal funds. They brought over food and spent time with him. They bathed Mike in love and comfort to help him deal with his pain.

Whether people are dealing with grief, financial difficulties, physical problems, or marital discord, we can come alongside to help. Sometimes God will direct us to help someone through the same trials that we have been through or are struggling with now. Other times, He will place us in situations where we can aid someone who is dealing with something we know little about. Either way, He will give us the privilege of touching lives —of believers and nonbelievers—and caring for them as representatives of His caring heart.

Have you ever considered where your strengths are in caring? Are you a good listener? Do you enjoy sharing your cooking skills with others? Do you relate especially well to mothers of preschoolers? Do you have a tender heart for the elderly?

God will place you where you can function for His glory. But we must be prepared to act when opportunities arise. Here are some suggestions:

- Set aside money as "help" funds to use when someone has a financial emergency.

- Take time monthly to care for needs of the lonely or elderly.

- Volunteer to care for the homeless, foster children, terminally ill patients, or another ministry that would fit your spiritual strengths.

- Spend time in the church nursery holding babies. Then get to know the babies' parents and find out what they need too.

As you study the following lessons, think about your commitment to caring and be open to letting God's Word inspire you to care for a particular person or group.

Unbounded Love

Jesus never asks anything of us that He didn't ask of Himself. And loving His enemies was the premiere example. He died for the sins of the whole world—even for the sins of His enemies, for those who would never accept His sacrifice. He loved that soldier who was pounding nails into His flesh. His heart was broken over the onlookers who were shouting insults at Him. Through His agony, He still paid attention to the words of the thieves hanging on either side of Him. With that kind of example before us, and His life within us, we *can* love our enemies. What kind of opposition are you facing? A neighbor who is hostile toward your children? A coworker who envies your position? A businessman who cheated you out of a substantial sum of money? Look to Jesus for the example and power of how to love.

His WORD: Luke 6:27–36

KNOWING *His* HEART

1. How should we treat our enemies (verses 27 and 28)?

2. How is selflessness demonstrated in verses 29–31?

3. Describe the actions of "sinners" in verses 32–34.

4. Why are Christians to respond differently from sinners (verse 35)?

KNOWING *My* HEART

1. How have you treated those who have hurt you?

2. How would people respond if you consistently lived out the Golden Rule (verse 31)?

3. What is the ultimate purpose of treating others, even our enemies, with kindness and mercy?

4. What do you think "reward" means in verse 35? How does this affect your motivation in your treatment of enemies?

My HEART IN *His* HANDS

"If ever a person deserved a shot at revenge, Jesus did. But he didn't take it. Instead he died for [His enemies]."

—MAX LUCADO

LESSON 12

Practical Generosity

In her allegory *Mountains of Spices*, Hannah Hurnard describes the importance of generosity. A girl, Grace and Glory, was sitting on Mountain of Love, where every piece of creation gave of itself. Fruit trees produced wonderful fruit; wildflowers gave sweetness and perfume. Majestic white peaks rose all around. But one lower peak was dark and spoiled—Black Mountain, where the enemy had planted weeds and ruined the land. "How can this evil be broken?" Grace and Glory asked the King. "Only self-giving and self-sharing can break the curse of evil roots," the King told her. "Generosity fulfills the royal law of love and restores harmony and righteousness." So together, the two of them bounded down Mountain of Love to the Black Mountain to spread generosity where it was so desperately needed.

His WORD: Matthew 25:31–40

KNOWING *His* HEART

1. Describe the picture given in verses 31–33. What do the two groups represent?

2. For what will the King praise believers in verses 34–36?

3. What response did the righteous have to the King's praise (verses 37–39).

4. Who were the recipients of these kindnesses? How does this relate to the King?

KNOWING *My* HEART

1. How are the needs described in verses 34–36 met today? In what ways is it different now than then?

2. Have you been the recipient of such practical generosity?

3. How do these verses affect your perspective on helping those in need?

4. Why do you think Christ identifies Himself with "the least of these"?

My HEART IN *His* HANDS

"The unlovely we may meet
Need our love the more.
Make us one, O love, we plead,
With men's sorrow and their need."
—HANNAH HURNARD

LESSON 13

Godly Compassion

Zechariah warned the Jewish people that what they did would have far-reaching influence—for good or for evil. He reminds them of how their ancestors failed to follow God or to repent of their sin. One day while Zechariah was praying, the Lord spoke to him about the hearts of the people. They had been given the task of rebuilding the temple after opposition caused the work to cease. But along with the physical structure, they were to build a spiritual temple in their hearts that would reflect God's heart. Compassion was a key component. Sometimes we think that our actions won't make much difference. Like the Jews, we can become so involved with erecting buildings that we neglect God's purpose for them—touching other lives for Him.

His WORD: Zechariah 7:8–10

KNOWING *His* HEART

1. What can you infer from the statement that the Lord came to Zechariah "again" (verse 8)?

2. What three attributes are we to show to one another (verse 9)?

3. What four types of needy people are we not to oppress (verse 10)?

4. How does verse 10 say we should regard others?

KNOWING *My* HEART

1. How do churches today supplant compassion with other goals?

2. When you were the recipient of justice, mercy, or compassion, how was the Spirit of Christ shown to you through these?

3. In what ways does society oppress widows, the fatherless, aliens, or the poor?

4. Ask God to reveal how you have fallen short regarding the last part of verse 10. Endeavor this week to obey this consistently.

My HEART IN *His* HANDS

"God of justice, you are King over all people, rich and poor alike. We praise you for your compassion for the needy and oppressed. Teach us to imitate your love, and help us to defend those who cannot defend themselves. Amen."
—PRAISE AND WORSHIP STUDY BIBLE

LESSON 14

Unlimited Encouragement

Television does not usually mix strength with encouragement. A large muscular man is normally portrayed as tough and insensitive. Like Rambo, he charges through life using his fists and probably shouting obscenities when things go wrong. He lives by his emotions rather than by cool sense. When caught in a corner, he lies, punches, and shoots his way out of trouble. But God shows us that encouragement takes great strength. When we are strong because of God's help, we can help others who are weak. We can put up with attacks against us because our hearts are held in God's hand. We care for those ignored by society because we can see them through God's eyes. Once again, Jesus is our example. He encouraged His disciples just before He was crucified because He knew how difficult the experience would be for them. That's the kind of strength we need!

His **WORD:** Romans 15:1–6

KNOWING *His* HEART

1. What are those who are strong called upon to do in verses 1 and 2?

2. Describe Christ's example to us in verse 3.

3. From verse 4, why were the Scriptures given to us?

4. What is the purpose of unity (verses 5 and 6)?

KNOWING *My* HEART

1. What can you do to please your neighbor "for his good" to build him up?

2. Who has been an encourager in your life? How?

3. In which areas are you strong? How can you use your strength to encourage others?

4. How can you help build a spirit of unity in your church?

My HEART IN *His* HANDS

"The beautiful thing about encouragement is that anyone can do it."

—CHARLES R. SWINDOLL

An Open Heart

Amy Carmichael experienced a deep change in her life when she was a teenager. On a gray, drizzling Sunday, when she and her two brothers left the church service, they saw an old, ragged woman struggling to carry a heavy bundle. "Let's help her," Amy urged impulsively. So they did. But then Amy became embarrassed to be seen with the dirty woman in front of other churchgoers. As they passed a fountain in a square, however, Amy heard a voice boom 1 Corinthians 3:12–14. No one else seemed to hear it. The verse challenged her to examine what she was doing for God. She was to serve God with works of gold and silver, not of hay and stubble. Soon, she began inviting neighborhood children to hear Bible lessons. She also began to work with the poor at the Belfast City Mission. It was the beginning of her lifelong work.

His **WORD:** Psalm 41:1; 82:3;
Proverbs 21:13; 31:20; Matthew 19:21

KNOWING *His* HEART

1. How is the godly woman described in Proverbs 31:20?

2. According to Psalm 82:3, how should we help those less fortunate?

3. What warning does Proverbs 21:13 give to those who disregard the needy?

4. What will the person receive who helps the poor and weak (Psalm 41:1; Matthew 19:21)?

KNOWING *My* HEART

1. How did both Dorcas and Amy exhibit open hearts?

2. Describe a time when you were needy. Who helped you? What did it mean to you?

3. How can you have an open heart toward the poor and needy?

4. What can you do to help local ministries that serve the poor and needy?

My HEART IN *His* HANDS

"*Come one, come all,*
To the Welcome Hall,
And come in your working clothes."

—AMY CARMICHAEL

PART 4

The Attitudes of Caring

Amy Carmichael was amazing. But she was just one of many single missionaries who considered their call from God to be more compelling than their families, country, and even marriage.

Another woman from the British Isles, who lived a little later than Amy, was Gladys Aylward. She had a heart for bringing the gospel to people outside her sphere of influence. She believed that God was calling her to China.

In the early 1930s, she made the rounds of mission agencies, but no one would accept her because of her poor academic record. (It may have been caused by a profound learning disability.) So she decided that if she couldn't obtain the approval of an established mission society, she would go on her own.

She knew of an elderly missionary widow in China who was

looking for someone to help her. Gladys saved until she had enough money to pay for a train ticket from London through Russia and into China. At the time, Russia was engaged in a border war with China, and Gladys ended up in the middle of the fighting. She eventually arrived at her destination, Yangcheng.

Facing severe loneliness, financial problems, and culture shock, Gladys carried on. She went from house to house teaching about Jesus. She refused to leave even when Japan attacked China and the war came to her area. Instead, she cared for the villagers embroiled in the fighting.

Like Amy, she noticed that the children were suffering the most. She assumed responsibility for dozens of war orphans. Eventually, the number swelled to one hundred. When Mao Tse Tung took over China, she was forced to leave. Then she went on to serve in Taiwan.

Later in life, Gladys received a lot of recognition for her self-less work in China. Although she didn't seek publicity, she became an international celebrity, speaking in many places, including America.

The Lord is not looking for someone with great talents, incredible riches, or outstanding charisma. He wants the heart of a woman, then He provides the opportunities for her to serve others. If we want to obey God, our caring attitude is essential. Gladys came from a working class family. She didn't have impeccable educational credentials, and she wasn't a gifted orator. Yet she touched the world with her dedication to Christ and her story of how God's love and caring could be spread through the hands of a humble woman.

Our only responsibility is to have the right attitude—then God will use us. We are to imitate Christ, be obedient to God's commands, serve others, and pay attention to their needs. It sounds simple, and it is. But we can only accomplish it as we place our caring heart in God's hands.

Imitate Christ

f you visit an elementary school classroom, you might hear this phrase used often: "Check your attitude!" It means something has gone wrong with the way someone's thinking, and it needs to be changed! Children aren't the only ones who need an attitude check. Adults do too! But many times we avoid considering what we do wrong, or become offended if anyone mentions a problem. But God has given us a sure way to analyze our attitude and keep it on the right track. Christ is our example; we are to imitate Him. Have you ever used a level when building or remodeling something? We know the item is placed correctly when the bubble floats to the very center. That's the way our lives function best too—centered on Christ. Through His example, we can make sure our caring attitude is "on the level."

His **WORD:** Philippians 2:1–11

KNOWING *His* HEART

1. Because of what we have received from Christ, what are we to do (verses 2–4)?

2. Although He was God, how did Christ demonstrate humility (verses 6 and 7)?

3. Why did God exalt Christ and give Him a name above every

name (verses 8 and 9)?

4. How will all mankind ultimately respond to the name of Jesus (verses 10 and 11)?

KNOWING *My* HEART

1. How has "being united with Christ" encouraged you and comforted you?

2. How can this attitude help you when you are caring for "the interests of others"?

3. Describe "the nature of a servant." What areas in your spirit are similar to a Christlike servant? What areas are not?

4. How can you exalt Christ in your worship times?

My HEART IN *His* HANDS

"Do you want to be blessed? Develop a servant's heart. If Jesus can step down from His glorious equality with God to become a man, and then further humble Himself to be a servant and wash the feet of twelve undeserving sinners—then humble Himself to die so horribly on our behalf, surely we ought to be willing to suffer any indignity to serve Him."

—JOHN MACARTHUR

LESSON 17

Be Obedient

Obey your elders" was a common teaching a few decades ago. Children learned to respect those in authority and those who had more experience. Today, we more often hear, "You can't make me do that. I have my rights!" That attitude is the opposite of obedience. Claiming our rights may be "legally" acceptable, but insisting on our own way is not God's plan. There is also a danger in disobedience. If you are traveling 65 mph down a four-lane freeway, you might want to squelch those feelings of "doing it my way." Instead, you will want to keep your car within those little white lines on the pavement. If you begin to drive in any lane you please whenever you want, you won't make it to your destination. But it is even more important to obey God's commands because they aren't merely physical laws, they are eternal.

His **WORD:** 1 John 5:1–5

KNOWING *His* **HEART**

1. How do we know that a person is born of God (verse 1)?

2. How do we show that we love the children of God (verse 2)?

3. What does verse 3 say about God's commands?

4. Who is it that overcomes the world (verses 4 and 5)?

KNOWING *My* HEART

1. Describe the relationship between love and obedience.

2. What are some commands God has given us on how we should treat others?

3. How can you better show God's love to your Christian brothers and sisters?

4. In which areas of your life do you need God's power to overcome the world?

My HEART IN *His* HANDS

"God wants to bring us to the place where what He tells us to do is not nearly as important as who He is who gives the order."

—JOY DAWSON

LESSON 18

Serve Others

The service industry is one of the largest in our country. And it's growing. Think of all the people who serve you: sales clerks, bank tellers, restaurant servers, flight attendants, nurses and doctors, etc. What kind of reputation do these people have as a result of their jobs? Some are held in high esteem, but most are discounted by those they serve. If you have ever worked as a waitress, you understand how demanding people can be and how little they appreciate what you do. Most sales clerks can tell stories of how customers cursed at them, called them names, or treated them disrespectfully. One reason why people who serve get treated this way is that our culture does not value servanthood. Instead, we prize honor and "doing it my way." But God values service; it is a high priority to Him. Serving others is a key element in godly caring.

His WORD: 1 Peter 4:8–11

KNOWING *His* HEART

1. How does love deal with the problem of sin (verse 8)?

2. What are some ways we are to show love (verses 9 and 10)?

3. How are we to speak, whether in public or private (verse 11)?

4. How does our serving in God's strength reflect on Him?

KNOWING *My* HEART

1. What specific things could you do to "offer hospitality to one another"?

2. What gifts do you have that you could use to serve and care for others?

3. How can changing your speaking habits better reflect your role as God's ambassador?

4. Describe a time when God received glory because of someone's faithfulness in serving others.

My HEART IN *His* HANDS

"Be generous with the different things God gave you, passing them around so all get in on it: if words, let it be God's words; if help, let it be God's hearty help."

—1 PETER 2 (*THE MESSAGE*)

LESSON 19

Pay Attention

Jesus tells us to love our enemy and to do good to those who are mean to us, to love our neighbors, to care for the helpless and needy, to love our brothers. In Deuteronomy, God extends our horizons not only to our brother's personal welfare, but to his belongings also. There is no excuse for the believer who "finds" his neighbors tools or "forgets" to give back a possession she borrowed. The only way those outside of God's family will understand the difference between the world system and God's love is if we show them. That's why it's essential to respect the possessions of others. Pay attention to what's important to those we bump elbows with each day. Did you borrow your coworker's expensive pen? Make sure you return it promptly. Did you see your neighbors' puppy slip its leash and run into the road? Knock on their door and inform them of the problem. Do it all in the name of the Lord.

His **WORD:** Deuteronomy 22:1–4

KNOWING *His* HEART

1. What types of possessions are we to pay attention to (verses 1–3)?

2. How are we to treat someone's possession that we find (verse 2)?

3. What are we repeatedly commanded not to do (verses 1,3,4)? Why?

4. In what ways is this passage similar to the parable of the Good Samaritan?

KNOWING *My* HEART

1. How important is it to consider the material needs of those around you?

2. Why does God want you to care about the possessions of others if you are in the position to do so?

3. What kinds of attitudes do people around you display regarding the possessions of others?

4. How will obeying this passage help your Christian witness?

My HEART IN *His* HANDS

"To serve our brother, to please him, to allow him his due and to let him live, is the way of self-denial, the way of the cross."

—DIETRICH BONHOEFFER

LESSON 20

Caring Prayer

Prayer is a natural result of godly caring. Peter prayed on behalf of Dorcas. Amy Carmichael was a woman of prayer. Arulai, one of her most faithful helpers at Dohnavur, led her sister, Mimosa, to Christ. Mimosa wanted to come to Dohnavur to study the Bible, but her father refused. Mimosa lived among Hindus, practicing her Christian faith as best she could. She was considered a pariah and had to marry a scoundrel. One day, she brought two of her four sons to Amy. She looked so haggard and wanted so desperately to stay. But she had to go back to save the other two sons, especially the oldest one. Amy continued to pour out her heart to God about Mimosa's situation. Then years later, Mimosa arrived with her sons and a niece, a neglected toddler. They all became a part of Dohnavur. Caring prayer had won out!

His **WORD:** Philippians 1:3–11

KNOWING *His* **HEART**

1. 1. How would you describe Paul's prayers in verse 4?

2. What is the reason for confidence given in verse 6?

3. What does verse 7 say about Paul's commitment to others?

4. What does Paul tell God about the saints in verses 3 and 8?

KNOWING *My* HEART

1. What do you think is the relationship between praying and caring?

2. What will happen to your heart of caring if you neglect prayer?

3. How can Amy's example encourage you in your prayer life?

4. List several items of caring prayer that you will implement beginning today.

My HEART IN *His* HANDS

"We don't need to press Him, as if we had to deal with an unwilling God."
—AMY CARMICHAEL

Discussion Guide

The following pages contain information to help you use the Bible studies in this Guide. If you are using the *Caring Heart* lessons as a group study, the answers to the questions will help your facilitator guide the discussion. If you are studying the lessons on your own, refer to the answers after you have finished the lesson.

Answers are given for the first section of questions, called "Knowing HIS Heart." These questions are objective searches through the lesson's Bible passage. The second section, "Knowing MY Heart," are personal application questions and are written to help you use the Bible truths in your everyday life. Therefore, these questions will pertain to your individual situations.

If you are leading a group, work through the first section more thoroughly. Then allow volunteers to give answers to the second section of questions. Some answers may be so personal that your group members will not want to express them aloud. Be sensitive to your group members' feelings in this area.

The Lord bless you are you apply the steps to wisdom in your life!

Part 1: The Heart of Caring

LESSON 1: CHRIST'S LOVE FOR US

1. Because God first loved us.

2. We prove we love God when we love our fellow Christians.

3. If he can't love someone he can see, how can he love someone he cannot see?

4. Whoever loves God must also love his brother.

LESSON 2: THE IMPORTANCE OF GENEROSITY

1. We will reap in proportion to what we have sown. Giving should come cheerfully from the heart. God will graciously provide all we need in every good work.

2. God supplies our needs and will enlarge our harvest in righteousness so that we can continue to be generous for His glory.

3. Supplying the needs of God's people and causing thanks to God.

4. People will praise God because we have lived out the gospel. They will see an example of God's grace through our life.

LESSON 3: A HEART OF LOVE

1. He was testing Jesus to see how well He knew the law.

2. "Love the Lord your God will all your heart, soul, strength, and mind, and love your neighbor as yourself."

3. It cost the Samaritan bandages, oil, wine, money, and time. He didn't expect anything in return.

4. To love our neighbor as ourselves, we should be merciful to those we meet and selflessly care for their needs.

LESSON 4: ACTS OF LOVE

1. Someone who is spiritually dead commits evil actions and hates his brother. Someone who has eternal life commits righteous actions and loves his brother.

2. We can meet the physical needs of others when we have the means to do so. We should love by our actions and in truth, not just with words.

3. It helps us know that we belong to the truth and it sets our hearts at rest in God's presence when our hearts condemn us.

4. We are to believe in the name of God's Son, Jesus Christ, and we are to love each other as He commanded us to do (with actions and in truth).

LESSON 5: THE ATTRACTIVENESS OF CARING

1. Dorcas was a disciple, a follower of Christ. She was consistently doing good to help others, especially the poor. She made robes and other clothing for widows.

2. Dorcas became ill and died. Her friends tended to her body, then sent some men to Peter to ask for help.

3. Peter could see all of the good deeds Dorcas had done because the widows were crying and holding the clothing she had made for them.

4. He raised her from the dead and presented her to those who loved her.

Part 2: The Role of Caring

LESSON 6: GOD'S LOVE AND COMPASSION

1. God heard his cry for mercy. God listened to him, so the psalmist knows that can call on Him forever.

2. He was entangled in the cords of death, the anguish of the grave came upon him, and he was overcome by trouble and sorrow.

3. God is gracious, righteous, and compassionate; He protects the simplehearted and saves those in need.

4. He can be at rest because the Lord has been good to him. And he can trust that God will take care of him in the future.

LESSON 7: CHRIST'S MINISTRY OF CARING

1. She had suffered from bleeding for twelve years. Many doctors had been unable to help her and she had spent all her money, only to get worse instead of better.

2. She believed she would be healed if only she could touch Him.

3. In the midst of a crowd, He could feel when one person in need touched His garment.

4. Jesus healed the woman of her affliction because of her faith in Him.

LESSON 8: OUR RESPONSIBILITY TO DO GOOD

1. We should restore the person gently, and be cautious not to fall into sin ourselves.

2. We should test our own actions and not compare ourselves to anyone else.

3. People reap what they sow. If a person sows to please her sinful nature, she will reap the destruction that comes with it. If a person sows to please the Spirit, she will reap eternal life.

4. If we don't become weary in doing good and give up, we will reap a harvest.

LESSON 9: THE ROLE OF SUFFERING AND COMFORT

1. Because God, the Father of compassion and the God of all comfort, has comforted us in our times of trouble.

2. Just as Christ's suffering flows over into our lives, so does His

comfort overflow in us.

3. The comfort we receive is not just for our benefit; it should also flow out to comfort others. Because we receive comfort from God when we are distressed, we can comfort others to help them patiently endure when they in turn suffer.

4. We share our sufferings and our comfort with each other.

LESSON 10: THE CARING PRINCIPLE

1. Peter found this paralytic man who had been bedridden for eight years. Peter told him that Christ had healed him, and the man got up immediately.

2. They knew of the kindness that Dorcas had showed in her life, and they knew of the miraculous power that God had demonstrated through Peter. They were hopeful that Peter could help Dorcas.

3. In answer to prayer, God works through His servants in a powerful and often miraculous way.

4. Word about this miracle spread around Joppa and many people came to believe in the Lord.

Part 3: The Acts of Caring

LESSON 11: UNBOUNDED LOVE

1. We are to love them, do good to them, bless them, and pray for them.

2. It shows selflessness when we are not consumed with demanding our rights, but are willing to generously share what we have with others.

3. Sinners love those who love them, do good to those who are good to them, and lend to others, expecting to be repaid in full.

4. Because God is kind to the ungrateful and wicked, we should be too. It helps people see something different about us, and reminds us that God is kind to us even when we are ungrateful.

LESSON 12: PRACTICAL GENEROSITY

1. The Lord will sit on His throne with all the people in front of Him. He will separate them as a shepherd separates the sheep from the goats. The sheep represent His children; the goats represent those who have rejected Christ.

2. For feeding Him when He was hungry; giving Him something to drink when He was thirsty; inviting Him in when He was a stranger; clothing Him when He was naked; looking after Him when He was sick; and visiting Him when He was in prison.

3. The righteous were puzzled about why the King thought they did all these things. They did not remember feeding, clothing, visiting, or doing anything else for him.

4. These acts were done to the least of the brothers of the King, but He considers a kindness done to them as a kindness done to Him.

LESSON 13: GODLY COMPASSION

1. The Lord has spoken to Zechariah before. He was a prophet of God.

2. True justice, mercy, and compassion.

3. Widows, the fatherless, aliens, and the poor.

4. We are not to think evil of each other in our hearts.

LESSON 14: UNLIMITED ENCOURAGEMENT

1. We are to bear with the failings of the weak. We are not to please ourselves, but to please our neighbors for their own good. We are to build them up.

2. Christ did not please Himself, but took upon Himself the insults that were meant to fall on us.

3. Everything that was written in the past was written to teach us, help us endure, and give us hope.

4. So that with one heart we may glorify the God and Father of our Lord Jesus Christ.

LESSON 15: AN OPEN HEART

1. She opens her arms to those who have less than she does. She offers help to those who have needs.

2. We should defend those who can't defend themselves (the weak and fatherless) and maintain the rights of those who can't stand up for their own rights (the poor and oppressed).

3. When they cry out to God, the Lord will not answer.

4. She receives blessing, deliverance in times of trouble, and treasure in heaven.

Part 4: The Attitudes of Caring

LESSON 16: IMITATE CHRIST

1. Be like-minded with Christ, having the same love; be one in spirit and purpose; don't act out of selfish ambition or vain conceit, but humbly consider others above ourselves and look to the interests of others.

2. Jesus humbled Himself by not seeking equality with God on

earth. He made Himself to be nothing, taking on the nature of a servant.

3. Because Christ humbled Himself and was obedient to the point of death on a cross.

4. Every knee will bow and every tongue will confess that Jesus Christ is Lord, to the glory of God the Father.

LESSON 17: BE OBEDIENT

1. Someone who is born of God believes that Jesus is the Christ, and loves other believers.

2. By loving and obeying God.

3. Obeying God's commands shows our love for Him. His commands are not burdensome.

4. Everyone who is born of God, who believes that Jesus is the Son of God.

LESSON 18: SERVE OTHERS

1. Love covers over a multitude of sins. This means that if we love people, we should overlook (forgive) their sins against us.

2. We are to offer hospitality without grumbling, to use whatever gifts we have to serve others, and to show God's grace.

3. We should speak thoughtfully, as one speaking the very words of God.

4. God will be praised through Jesus Christ and He will receive glory and power.

LESSON 19: PAY ATTENTION

1. Our brother's ox, sheep, or donkey, his cloak, or anything he loses. We are to take care of anything that belongs to others.

2. If we are unable to return it, we are to take care of it until he

comes for it. Then we should give it back to him.

3. Do not ignore it. We must show a heart of caring, and do for others what we would want someone to do for us.

4. We are instructed not to pass by but to pay attention to the need; show concern for the person; care for the possession as if it were own, including incurring expense; and not expect reimbursement.

LESSON 20: CARING PRAYER

1. Paul's prayers for the saints were all-inclusive, regular, and filled with joy.

2. Christ is carrying on the good work He started in believers until He comes again.

3. He cares for them deeply, even thinking of them when he is in chains and defending the gospel.

4. Paul would like their love—for Christ and for others—to deepen; their discernment to be clear; and their actions to demonstrate the fruit of righteousness that comes only from Jesus.

Beginning Your Journey of Joy

These four principles are essential in beginning a journey of joy.

One—*God loves you and created you to know Him personally.*

God's Love
"God so loved the world that He gave His one and only Son, that whoever believes in Him shall not perish but have eternal life" (John 3:16).

God's Plan
"Now this is eternal life: that they may know you, the only true God, and Jesus Christ, whom you have sent" (John 17:3).

What prevents us from knowing God personally?

Two—*People are sinful and separated from God, so we cannot know Him personally or experience His love.*

People are Sinful
"All have sinned and fall short of the glory of God" (Romans 3:23).

People were created to have fellowship with God; but, because of our own stubborn self-will, we chose to go our own independent way and fellowship with God was broken. This self-will, characterized by an attitude of active rebellion or passive indifference, is an evidence of what the Bible calls sin.

People are Separated

"The wages of sin is death" [spiritual separation from God] (Romans 6:23).

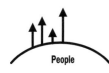

This diagram illustrates that God is holy and people are sinful. A great gulf separates the two. The arrows illustrate that people are continually trying to reach God and establish a personal relationship with Him through our own efforts, such as a good life, philosophy, or religion—but we inevitably fail.

The third principle explains the only way to bridge this gulf…

Three—*Jesus Christ is God's only provision for our sin. Through Him alone we can know God personally and experience His love.*

He Died In Our Place

"God demonstrates His own love toward us, in that while we were yet sinners, Christ died for us" (Romans 5:8).

He Rose from the Dead

"Christ died for our sins…He was buried…He was raised on the third day according to the Scriptures…He appeared to Peter, then to the twelve. After that He appeared to more than five hundred…" (1 Corinthians 15:3–6).

He Is the Only Way to God

"Jesus said to him, 'I am the way, and the truth, and the life; no one comes to the Father but through Me'" (John 14:6).

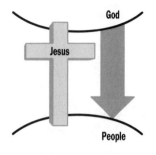

This diagram illustrates that God has bridged the gulf that separates us from Him by sending His Son, Jesus Christ, to die on the cross in our place to pay the penalty for our sins.

It is not enough just to know these three truths…

Four—We must individually receive Jesus Christ as Savior and Lord; then we can know God personally and experience His love.

We Must Receive Christ
"As many as received Him, to them He gave the right to become children of God, even to those who believe in His name" (John 1:12).

We Receive Christ Through Faith
"By grace you have been saved through faith; and that not of yourselves, it is the gift of God; not as a result of works that no one should boast" (Ephesians 2:8,9).

When We Receive Christ, We Experience a New Birth
(Read John 3:1–8.)

We Receive Christ By Personal Invitation
[Christ speaking] "Behold, I stand at the door and knock; if anyone hears My voice and opens the door, I will come in to him" (Revelation 3:20).

Receiving Christ involves turning to God from self (repentance) and trusting Christ to come into our lives to forgive us of our sins and to make us what He wants us to be. Just to agree intellectually that Jesus Christ is the Son of God and that He died on the cross for our sins is not enough. Nor is it enough to have an emotional experience. We receive Jesus Christ by faith, as an act of our will.

These two circles represent two kinds of lives:

Self-Directed Life
S – Self is on the throne
† – Christ is outside the life
● – Interests are directed by self, often resulting in discord and frustration

Christ-Directed Life
† – Christ is in the life and on the throne
S – Self is yielding to Christ
● – Interests are directed by Christ, resulting in harmony with God's plan

Which circle best represents your life?
Which circle would you like to have represent your life?

The following explains how you can receive Christ:

You Can Receive Christ Right Now by Faith Through Prayer
(Prayer is talking with God)

God knows your heart and is not so concerned with your words as He is with the attitude of your heart. The following is a suggested prayer:

> *Lord Jesus, I want to know You personally. Thank You for dying on the cross for my sins. I open the door of my life and receive You as my Savior and Lord. Thank You for forgiving my sins and giving me eternal life. Take control of the throne of my life. Make me the kind of person You want me to be.*

Does this prayer express the desire of your heart?

If it does, I invite you to pray this prayer right now, and Christ will come into your life, as He promised.

How to Know That Christ Is in Your Life
Did you receive Christ into your life? According to His promise in Revelation 3:20, where is Christ right now in relation to you?

Christ said that He would come into your life. Would He mislead you? On what authority do you know that God has answered your prayer? (The trustworthiness of God Himself and His Word.)

The Bible Promises Eternal Life to All Who Receive Christ

"The witness is this, that God has given us eternal life, and this life is in His Son. He who has the Son has the life; he who does not have the Son of God does not have the life. These things I have written to you who believe in the name of the Son of God, in order that you may know that you have eternal life" (1 John 5:11–13).

Thank God often that Christ is in your life and that He will never leave you (Hebrews 13:5). You can know on the basis of His promise that Christ lives in you and that you have eternal life from the very moment you invite Him in. He will not deceive you.

An important reminder…

Feelings Can Be Unreliable

You might have expectations about how you should feel after placing your trust in Christ. While feelings are important, they are unreliable indicators of your sincerity or the trustworthiness of God's promise. Our feelings change easily, but God's Word and His character remain constant. This illustration shows the relationship among **fact** (God and His Word), **faith** (our trust in God and His Word), and our **feelings**.

Fact: The chair is strong enough to support you.

Faith: You believe this chair will support you, so you sit in it.

Feeling: You may or may not feel comfortable in this chair, but it continues to support you.

The promise of God's Word, the Bible—not our feelings—is our authority. The Christian lives by faith (trust) in the trustworthiness of God Himself and His Word.

Now That You Have Entered Into a Personal Relationship With Christ

The moment you received Christ by faith, as an act of your will, many things happened, including the following:

- Christ came into your life (Revelation 3:20; Colossians 1:27).

- Your sins were forgiven (Colossians 1:14).

- You became a child of God (John 1:12).

- You received eternal life (John 5:24).

- You began the great adventure for which God created you (John 10:10; 2 Corinthians 5:17; 1 Thessalonians 5:18).

Can you think of anything more wonderful that could happen to you than entering into a personal relationship with Jesus Christ? Would you like to thank God in prayer right now for what He has done for you? By thanking God, you demonstrate your faith.

To enjoy your new relationship with God...

Suggestions for Christian Growth

Spiritual growth results from trusting Jesus Christ. "The righteous man shall live by faith" (Galatians 3:11). A life of faith will enable you to trust God increasingly with every detail of your life, and to practice the following:

G   *Go* to God in prayer daily (John 15:7).

R   *Read* God's Word daily (Acts 17:11); begin with the Gospel of John.

O   *Obey* God moment by moment (John 14:21).

W   *Witness* for Christ by your life and words (Matthew 4:19; John 15:8).

T   *Trust* God for every detail of your life (1 Peter 5:7).

H   *Holy Spirit*—allow Him to control and empower your daily life and witness (Galatians 5:16,17; Acts 1:8; Ephesians 5:18).

Fellowship in a Good Church

God's Word admonishes us not to forsake "the assembling of ourselves together" (Hebrews 10:25). Several logs burn brightly together, but put one aside on the cold hearth and the fire goes out. So it is with your relationship with other Christians. If you do not belong to a church, do not wait to be invited. Take the initiative; call the pastor of a nearby church where Christ is honored and His Word is preached. Start this week, and make plans to attend regularly.

Resources

My Heart in His Hands: Renew a Steadfast Spirit Within Me. Spring—renewal is everywhere; we are reminded to cry out to God, "Renew a steadfast spirit within me." The first of four books in Vonette Bright's devotional series, this book will give fresh spiritual vision and hope to women of all ages. ISBN 1-56399-161-6

My Heart in His Hands: Set Me Free Indeed. Summer—a time of freedom. Are there bonds that keep you from God's best? With this devotional, a few moments daily can help you draw closer to the One who gives true freedom. This is the second of four in the devotional series. ISBN 1-56399-162-4

My Heart in His Hands: I Delight Greatly in My Lord. Do you stop to appreciate the blessings God has given you? Spend time delighting in God with book three in this devotional series. ISBN 1-56399-163-2

My Heart in His Hands: Lead Me in the Way Everlasting. We all need guidance, and God is the ultimate leader. These daily moments with God will help you to rely on His leadership. The final in the four-book devotional series. ISBN 1-56399-164-0

My Heart in His Hands: Bible Study Guides. Designed to complement the four devotional books in this series, the Bible Study Guides allow a woman to examine God's Word and gain perspective on the issues that touch her life. Each study highlights a biblical character and includes an inspirational portrait of a woman who served God. Available in 2002:

A Renewed Heart (1-56399-176-4)
A Nurturing Heart (1-56399-177-2)
A Woman's Heart (1-56399-178-0)
A Free Heart (1-56399-179-9)
A Wise Heart (1-56399-180-2)
A Caring Heart (1-56399-181-0)

The Joy of Hospitality: Fun Ideas for Evangelistic Entertaining. Co-written with Barbara Ball, this practical book tells how to share your faith through hosting barbecues, coffees, holiday parties, and other events in your home. ISBN 1-56399-057-1

The Joy of Hospitality Cookbook. Filled with uplifting scriptures and quotations, this cookbook contains hundreds of delicious recipes, hospitality tips, sample menus, and family traditions that are sure to make your entertaining a memorable and eternal success. Co-written with Barbara Ball. ISBN 1-56399-077-6

The Greatest Lesson I've Ever Learned. In this treasury of inspiring, real-life experiences, twenty-three prominent women of faith share their "greatest lessons." Does God have faith- and character-building lessons for you in their rich, heart-warming stories? ISBN 1-56399-085-7

Beginning Your Journey of Joy. This adaptation of the *Four Spiritual Laws* speaks in the language of today's women and offers a slightly feminine approach to sharing God's love with your neighbors, friends, and family members. ISBN 1-56399-093-8

These and other fine products from *New**Life*** Publications are available from your favorite bookseller or by calling (800) 235-7255 (within U.S.) or (407) 826-2145, or by visiting www.newlifepubs.com.